The First Ten Steps

- Ten proven steps to build a solid foundation for your ebook using free social networking

by International Bestselling Independent Fantasy Author,

M. R. Mathias

M. R. Mathias

Step One

A Good Book

This is an obvious step, and it is first because this is part of the free preview. It is the most important step though. No amount of advertising or promotion will make a bad book good. A perfect edit and an awesome cover will not make a bad book good. Reviews from ten of your best friends, or ten complete strangers will not make a bad book good, either. Those things might make a book sell, but a bad story will remain a bad story, and that means at some point things will fizzle away. However, a good, solid book will grow steadily with these steps, and a great book might grow exponentially into a huge bestseller.

- Readers are your best friend. Please the readers, and the critics will follow.

That means you must know who your readers are, and what other books are doing well in your genre. Judge your book's look and content by its peers, and be honest with yourself. If you don't tell yourself the truth, who will? However, do not judge your books sales by its peers. Time and genre have a lot to do with early sales. Watching others at this stage is pointless, save for observing what is working for them.

Your book doesn't have to be a great book, just a good, solid book, with a good plot and an interesting story line. Oh, and a good edit.

I didn't say a perfect edit; I said a good edit.

There are hundreds of thousands of readers out there. If your book is good, some will love it, some will hate it, and over time a bunch of people will buy it. The trick is getting it out there so that people will see it and know that it's there.

The rest of the steps in this book will tell you ways I have used and observed as "working well" to generate attention and sales of eBooks from **new** authors.

Some books of this type are out there, but they were published by well-known authors who didn't start from scratch. These **Ten Steps** are for the unknown self publisher with their first or second indie book. Most of these methods are FREE.

If you want to succeed as an author without big money publishing behind you, laying the **foundation** for yourself and your first book is one of the most important things you can do. Lay the groundwork properly, and you can build a rock solid platform.

My credentials can be found on the sell pages for my M. R. Mathias fantasy books at Amazon, where several of them reside in the top 100 bestseller lists for their genre. Starting with no name recognition and less computer skills than money, I sold over 50k ebooks my very first year. If you follow my steps and devote a few hours a week to promotion, you too can become a known author and make steady money selling your ebooks, but only if the books are good.

Step Two

Look at your Book Cover

I am the first to say "don't judge a book by its cover." I paid a small fortune for my most recent cover because I learned that it does help sales, and in ways you are not aware of yet. Ignoring the cover is stupid. Again, the cover doesn't have to be great, just a good, traditional looking book cover.

- GVTgrafix.com is one resource (that's an email, not a website.) GVT is a cover designer for hire. He is reasonable. There are sites like deviantart.com and the clipart sites like iStockphoto where you can find the image you want. Look at other books and use your best judgment. A solid colored rectangle with some off colored text will work for a "How To" book, but it won't draw people in as well as some good art and graphics will. That's just the way it is.

Part of the job you have just taken on as promoter/publisher of your own book is generating content for posts, such as tweets, and Facebook promotions. Using good cover art generates a lot of profile visits. You can post your cover on Facebook and/or a blog post and ask for input about it. You can then tweet the link to that post a few times a week on Twitter. Using Twitter will be covered in later steps. The point is that a good digital book cover helps in more than just the obvious way. It can be a conversation piece, and it can draw the eye of a potential reader that might look over a plain cover.

Step Three

My good book, with its good cover is uploaded.

What do I do now?

First, you make a text or word file called "Link File". Copy and paste the links to your books "sell pages" in there. This will be a handy reference when making tweets and posting about your book. I personally only upload my books to Amazon, Smashwords, and Pubit. At Smashwords, I just decline the Amazon and Barnes & Noble options. Smashwords is very important for three main reasons: the Sony Reader Store, the Apple iStore, and Borders/Kobo store.

You can upload only to Smashwords. They will distribute your ebook to Amazon and B&N too. Smashwords pays quarterly. This has nothing to do with the purpose of this book, but it does have to do with the way you make your money. There are ways to advertise that are not free, and if you want to use the profits from your book to advertise, you need to get paid monthly. Thus I use Amazon KDP for Kindle, and Pubit for Barnes & Noble. I use Smashwords for everything else.

You probably have Twitter and Facebook accounts already. What about Goodreads? What about Wattpad? You need all of these, and you need the account name in a variation similar to your pen name, like "M_R_Mathias" or "Author_MRMathias" for M. R. Mathias. My wattpad id is MRMathias. You will have a full author's page at Goodreads. Your pen name is your brand, and brand name is important in social media marketing. It's better if people recognize you. Try to use the same one everywhere. I didn't; I used @DahgMahn for my twitter name. That threw people off until they read *The Sword and the Dragon*, then it made sense to them. It slowed down growth for a while, but luckily I got over that hump.

You also need to join http://www.independentauthornetwork.com/index.html or a similar author group. This is a valuable resource and will fit neatly into the later steps. This is a suggestion. IAN (Independent Authors Network) isn't free, but it is affordable, and it will pay for itself over and over in your first year.

For all of these accounts you will need a good Authors Photo in .jpeg, along with a neat and concise bio. Don't write a big bio. No one wants to hear that much about you. Look around Goodreads and at the Amazon authors pages to see what is working with the genre/authors you follow.

Therefore, Step Three is to join:

- Facebook
- Twitter
- Goodreads
- Wattpad
- Genre related forum groups or message boards ie: Horror fan club, Mystery Lovers, Nook Boards, etc...
- Independent Authors Network (If you want to spare the expense)
- If you have a blog this will be used too. If not, make one using your author's name, or the name of the book you are promoting. .blogspot.com has free sites available. I use a yahoo website that I pay around $100 a year for.

Add the links to your new homepages/blog pages to the "Link File" you made and label them well. You will use them a lot.

Step Four

My social media accounts are made.

What do I do now?

We are going to get started with some simple, basic, free promotion that needs to be tended on a regular basis. Set aside ten minutes a day for this stuff, and then we will expand into more involved promotion as the steps progress.

Copy your books Amazon sales page link from your "Link File" and paste it into a new Facebook status update. Your cover should appear and you will have room to type about the link. Type something like "Hey guys, stop by and read the free preview of my new book," or if you are lucky and have a good review, say "Come look at the new review my book just received." I'm to the point where I just add the link and type "New Review."

In the first comment of the post type: "You can follow me @Dahgmahn on Twitter." Mention your Twitter handle in every post you can. Twitter will eventually become your best friend.

The next day on Facebook, post a different link. Post the link to your Goodreads homepage and add the text "Stop by and friend me at Goodreads." This seems obvious, but you have to get into a routine. Post something everyday around the same time at the same places. Your Goodreads page will have info about you, and **your new book will automatically absorb into the Goodreads book system** (a few days after it goes live on Amazon and Smashwords.) This is very important, because the Sony Reader Store uses your book's Goodreads reviews on its sell pages. You want a clean, spiffy Goodreads page. When people on Facebook click the link you posted, they will learn from Goodreads what books you like, along with information about you and the book you wrote. In your bio at Goodreads, be sure to add that you can be found @DahgMahn on Twitter and/or put a link to your blog or webpage.

Spend some time at Goodreads each day, too. Search the quotes there, or other peoples books. Rate books you've read. Your Goodreads page can be linked to your Facebook page via the Facebook Goodreads app. and it will show that you liked this book, or added a quote from one of your favorites authors. By using the app you are effectively posting at two places at once. People who have similar tastes will friend you or comment on your posts. **Goodreads has dozens of genre book clubs that welcome new authors. JOIN THEM.**

Do Not Abuse the posting rules at these club pages. Find out what they allow and then post your book info in the designated area. Join in the conversation without pushing your book too hard. If you say something interesting, people will click on your name and that will take them to your profile.

- Goodreads also has an option to share what you do on Twitter. Use this every time you can.

These simple actions will give you more things to tweet about, or tweet them for you, and these actions set a tone for people who visit your page to see what you are into. They also build up the foundation we talked about earlier. Every post gets seen by a few people; some by hundreds. After a few months you will no longer be an unknown author and along the way, you will have gained several new friends and fans. You will also have built a Goodreads profile full of interesting content.

This is a slow building process. Do not expect immediate results.

A recap of Step Four:

Post links to your book's sale pages and your website/social media pages; a few Facebook posts, a few Goodreads posts, and a few tweets about those posts **each and every day**. Get into a cycle.

Step Five

I started using my social media accounts.

What do I do now?

Now we are going fishing for readers. To catch fish, we need bait. Readers don't like minnows, but they can't resist a good read. We want several types of bait. To catch a reader, we need free content. If your book has an action sequence or a gripping bit of drama, copy the best 4-8 pages, or even a chapter. Paste it into the "My Writing" section of your Goodreads page. Options to link to the source novel's Goodreads page are clear and easy to use. (Your book will have a Goodreads page weather you want it to or not. All Amazon/B&N/Smashwords books have a Goodreads page)

Take the exact same content you just copied and post it into your writing at Wattpad. You can add the cover there too, and select the option where they promote your work. (They link it on other pages within Wattpad and other reading sites)

These posted chunks of your writing will now be your **Samples**. You can make more than one. The first 10% of your book is automatically free at Amazon for kindle users to sample. Why not make the same 10% available free at Goodreads and Wattpad? At Smashwords you can set the length of your free sample. If your sample is good, people will go read a few chapters of your book online before they even know what they are doing. Then they are hooked.

Wattpad writing posts can be read by Wattpad subscribers on their cell phone via the Wattpad app. I don't know how it works, but it works. They have a loyal following. My flash fiction and short stories there have been read several thousand times each. The count is posted to the right of the stories. The tweet and share buttons are on the left. Put links to your book's sell pages and twitter at the end of all of those posts. That means the people who like what they just read can click the next link and buy the book, or maybe sample another item. It's all free and a really great way to get real readers into your work.

I will tell you exactly what to do with these samples later. As always, paste the links and clear labels to the sample posts in your "Link File."

The next reader bait is just plain old FREE content that is or isn't relevant to your book. I suggest a short story or a piece of flash fiction, or both. If you don't have anything written, then find a character in your book and write a tale about them that would make people want to know more. It can be a short piece, like my "Blood of Coldfrost" that introduces the characters in my fantasy trilogy in two gripping pages. It is at my Wattpad and Goodreads pages, and is a prime example of teasing a novel with short, free content. I am going to include it at the end of this step as an example. Take the time to read it. If you can write something like that, then you are well on your way to the next level. Post these flash fiction pieces and short stories at Goodreads and Wattpad, and save the links in your growing "Link File."

**Example of Flash Fiction:

The Blood of Coldfrost (A Wardstone Short)

Copyright 2010 by M.R. Mathias

The concussive "whoomp" of an exploding oil keg brought the encampment awake. A ball of flame roiled skyward, bathing the sparkling tundra of Coldfrost in an orange-yellow glow. Men were scrambling. Large, mannish forms, more feral than not, darted about the shadows unchecked. The battle roar of a Breed beast cut through the frigid night as it brought an ax down into the head of a Westland Captain who was emerging from his tent. Flames danced crazily and threw wild shadows about the chaos. From somewhere across the crunchy snow covered terrain, the shouts of a fervent sergeant rang out in an attempt to generate some sort of order among the terrified men.

In the Royal Pavilion, Mikahl was trying desperately to get his king's armor fastened. They had been in Coldfrost for days, hunting and corralling the wild breed beasts that came out of the mountains to feed on Westlander flesh. Even in the heated pavilion, it was so cold that Mikahl's fingers felt like giant sausages. Mikahl hated the cold. Coldfrost was bitter, but he was the King's Squire, and he would have rather cut off his own head than disappoint good King Balton. Determined, he ground his jaw tight with effort, fumbled the stiff leather straps through the buckles, and cinched them tight.

"You'll be stay'n out of it, Mik." The king stood and twisted his frame to get the ornate plated chest piece to settle. His visage was one of savage determination. Even inside the tent his breath came out in great clouds of steam. "Watch over the horses. If one of them fargin beasts comes at ya, remember your drills."

Outside the tent a man screamed out, his horrible voice cut over the din of battle. King Balton Collum winced at the sound of the agony, then pulled his infamous sword out of its sheath. Forgetting his helmet, he threw the scabbard to the side, and charged out into the freezing silver moonlight. The blade of his ancient weapon radiated an icy shade of blue as he went, but Ironspike's potent length swiftly graduated to the raging color of blood when the king put it to use.

Mikahl came out behind King Balton and darted around the pavilion to the canvas stall that was erected for the animals. He turned back just in time to see Ironspike's blade flash with a pulse of blinding energy. Screams of pain and fear erupted from man and beast alike as the flare filled the world full of blinding white radiance.

No breed beasts came for the horses, so Mikahl watched the battle waging out beyond the gray expanse of ice between him and the main encampment. Lord Gregory, the Lion Lord of Westland, was in a tangle with one of the ten foot tall creatures. The beast was trying to sink its finger long teeth into the Lion Lord, but finding it no easy

15

task. A pair of men danced around the combatants frantically. Every so often, one of them would dart in and jab his weapon into the breed beast's side.

Not far away, the Royal Wizard blasted at the creatures with streaking, lavender pulses of magical force. Pael looked insane with his wide open eyes, over clenched jaws, and his egg-shaped alabaster head. His charge, Prince Glendar, was calling out orders to a troop of men that surrounded a hand full of the breed. Mikahl wanted desperately to raise his old iron sword with them, but he wouldn't betray the king's order.

It ended when Duke Fairchild and his huntsmen came thundering in from the other camp on their warhorses. The Breed beasts were no match for the Duke's competent cavalry. With Lord Gregory's might and Ironspike's angry power thrown in the skirmish, the savage beasts were soon brought to bear.

After they were corralled, Pael spelled them into a stupor. In the morning, the men who were left alive herded them across the icy shallows, out onto the glacial Island with the others of their kind. King Balton then drove Ironspike's dragon-forged steel into the ice and let its power surge forth. A boundary was formed. The glassine field hummed and crackled with the power that would hold it in place for all of time. The Battle of Coldfrost was over. The feral Breed could no longer ravage the mountain herds or rape and pillage in the north.

One of the creatures stared at Mikahl from across the icy flow that separated the Island from the rest of the world. Mikahl couldn't help but wonder what the creatures would eat. The prison the beasts were just confined to was nothing more than a solid slab of ice. A glance around the encampment at the crimson stained tundra, and the gore strewn remains of his company hardened Mikahl to their dismal fate. *Let them starve.* He had no idea that someday he would have to face them again, but he would. When that came to pass, good King Balton would be long dead from Pael's traitorous poison.

Mikahl noticed one of his favorite sparring partners lying half shredded in the snow, and forced back a tear. He took Ironspike back from his King and dutifully ran to the pavilion to put it back into its sheath. The battlefield was so saturated with blood that his boots left a trail of footprints across the carpeted floor of the king's quarters. In all of his days, throughout all of the wild adventures his grand destiny would bring him, Mikahl would never forget the Battle of Coldfrost.

He would never forget the blood.

Thus ends The Blood of Coldfrost (A Wardstone Short) by M.R. Mathias

The Battle of Coldfrost took place a few years before "**The Sword and the Dragon**" begins

"**The Sword and the Dragon**" by M.R. Mathias is a 235,300 word (700 page) epic fantasy masterpiece,

with a 300 page free preview available now at this link: http://www.smashwords.com/books/view/22793

And DON'T MISS:

"**Kings, Queens, Heroes, & Fools**" – The Wardstone Trilogy Book II

Both novels are available now.

See how the info at the end leads the reader to a larger sample? When you make your free samples and short story posts ALLWAYS leave the reader with a way to immediately find more content. I put this piece on Goodreads, Wattpad, and uploaded it as its own eBook to Smashwords. The cover is terrible, but it is available for free download now at B&N, the iStore, Diesel eBooks, Sony, etc.... It can be read from a

PC screen on Goodreads, Wattpad and a few fantasy message board sites. It has been read well over 35k times. That is free publicity by definition. If you read the story, you know I am right.

This one story has about 13 different links for various sites, devices, and stores. I can tweet about it every day and go two weeks without tweeting the same link. Getting a grip on twitter is the next step.

Step Five recap:

Post samples, short stories, and short "flash" fiction on Goodreads and Wattpad.

Step Six

I posted samples, and other content at Goodreads and Wattpad.

What do I do now?

You are just about ready to explode onto the scene, but you need to grow your Twitter followers. This is a simple but tedious process, unless you have an automated system. I don't want anyone to break Twitter's rules, so I will say nothing more than this: If you Google "auto tweeter," you will find a ton of different options, from free to very expensive. Some operate with twitters blessing, others do not. This is not necessary, but if you find the right one and figure it out, it will help.

Even if you do not join the Independent Authors Network, you can use some of the free resources they provide. Search the site. On your twitter account search "#ian1". The list of tweets you will see are from authors using the IAN hash tag. There are several book related hash tags and more evolving every day. #BookLook, #ReadThis, #Kindle, #Nook, #sony, #iPad, #BookReview, and #Review are just a few of the many available. Search all of these and follow as many author related users you can. They will follow you back. They will retweet your tweets, too, and especially if you retweet theirs.

A moment to explain hash tags. When you tag your tweet it goes into a list with all the tweets that share that tag. If you put 5 hash tags in your tweet, it will go into all 5 lists. People searching for an eBook can search each hash tag list for samples.

I suggest following 50-100 people every day on twitter. About twenty-five percent of them will follow you back. Before long you will be tweeting to several hundred people, some of which will retweet your tweets to several more hundred people, and so on, and so on... Thus Twitter is one of your best friends.

I do realize that time isn't always on your side. You can find a famous author that writes in your genre on Twitter and look at the list of people who follow them. You can go down that list in a few short minutes clicking the follow button. It takes about 3 minutes to get 100 of them.

Another Twitter tip is the "auto follow back" and "auto thank you message." If you follow me on Twitter, my tweet deck auto sends a thank you message:

"Thanks for following. If you'd like to find out more about me and the fantasy novels I write, visit: www.mrmathias.com"

This is a great introduction. It isn't original. It is used by millions of Twitterers, but it is very effective if the link leads the user to interesting content. These auto tweeters messengers are available everywhere online. Use them at your own risk.

*Tweeting Tip: Hash tags

- Put the hash tag #RT at the end of your book tweets. With retweeting, a single tweet can potentially reach millions of people. #RT tells others you would like them to retweet your post.
- Here is an example of a well devised book tweet:

‘"The Royal Dragoneers' 400pgs of non-stop #dragon #fantasy #action for #kindle! by M.R.Mathias http://t.co/sQcobxcvia @Amazon #iPad #RT "

I made it by clicking on the "share" button on the book's Amazon page. To do this, select "like." Then click the Twitter icon, and a tweet will appear. You can manipulate it to suit your needs. Just keep the link and the "via @Amazon." On Twitter, when someone clicks on these types of Amazon Tweets, a mini version of your Amazon sell page will appear while the user is still in twitter.

Step Six Recap:

Grow friend and follower numbers on Twitter daily. This is one of the **Most Important** things you can do.

Step Seven

I now have followers and friends. My free content is posted.

What do I do now?

Now you are ready to put **YOU** in reader's faces.

Of the social media sites you joined, some are hosting sites and others are promotion sites. This is my own crude terminology. Let me explain.

Hosting sites: Goodreads, Wattpadd, Blogs. They let you upload writing, quotes, and other text files, and they display them permanently for other users to visit and comment on.

Promotion type sites: Facebook and Twitter have a real-time feed that trail your recent post down the stream. Only your friends and followers see these posts unless they "share" or "retweet" it with their friends.

We want to post the Hosted samples and story links into the promotion sites. We maximize this process by posting different content on given days. These are an ever changing phenomenon. These few are here to stay.

Every Sunday is #SampleSunday on Twitter. Post all of your Goodreads sample links in a tweet with the #SampleSunday and #RT hash tag. Then, post the Wattpad links of the same samples on Facebook and just say "For Sample Sunday a few pages from Ch. 22" or "My Sample Sunday offering is here: http//blahblahblah".

Sample Sunday is for your larger samples. Twitter users search #SampleSunday, and the list that unfolds for them is full of writing samples every week. Don't tweet your sample link out more than 3 times in a day, and change the wording of the tweet slightly between the three tweets. This will keep you from violating Twitters policy on repeating Tweets.

Saturday is Short Story Saturday, or #SSS. Saturday you tweet out the links to your Goodreads short story posts, and you post your Wattpad links at Facebook. Remember, your book link, website, and Twitter handle are at the end of all of your Sample/Story files. Anyone who likes what they read can find your book or site. This is effective, and also where the tide will turn in your favor, if you have been building your foundation.

#WW is Writer Wednesday. Search it, and you will see how it works. Authors tweet out other authors and everybody follows each other. It's a great way to gain followers.

Here is an example:

"#WW must follows @DahgMahn @rynedp @MrStubbsSays @BookReTweeter"

This is from a user and the point is to put his/her favorite Twitter users out there for others to follow. When you see one of these tweets from a user you know, follow the users listed in the tweet. Just click and follow. If it is a good friend then retweet the tweet for them. Remember, about 25% of the people you follow will follow you back.

Friday is #FridayFlash. Obviously, you post Tweets with links to your flash fiction pieces from Wattpad and Goodreads on twitter just like you did on Sunday.

*Important tips – **Alternate each week.** One week post Goodreads links on Twitter and Wattpad links on Facebook. The next week, post

Wattpad links on Twitter, and Goodreads links on Facebook. This avoids link repetition, and also spreads your profiles around. Also, add new content. Take a new sample from your book, and write a new flash story every now and then.

Recap of Step Seven:

Use Twitter days: #SampleSunday #ShortStorySaturday #SSS #FridayFlash #WW to distribute your samples and free content. Use other hash tags such as #ComingOfAge #Mystery and #Thriller to have your tweet listed in those tag streams

*Note – Your follower numbers and friends should be growing now, as well as your sales. **Do Not Stop Your Posting Cycle** (unless your last name is Hocking.)

Step Eight

I have more followers and friends. My content is OUT THERE.

What do I do now?

Mainly, you keep up the cycle of posting and tweeting. As you get new reviews, post them to Facebook and tweet them. This has become very easy with the addition of tweet buttons to everything on the web. Take the time to tweet your favorite blogs, and always retweet fellow authors. Reciprocal tweeting is key to success in this system. **Do Your Part Daily.**

You'll be followed by, and following, a bunch of book bloggers by now. You want to start filling out blog interview question forms and offering free copies of your book for review (via the Smashwords coupon system or Amazon gifting). When you visit someone's blog, find the tweet button and take the ten seconds it takes to put them out there. They might just return the favor with a retweet or a mention on the blog. **Twitter Karma is good thing to have.**

Submission guidelines for reviews can be found on the homepage of most blogs.

This is where having a group of retweeting authors like the Independent Authors Network behind you comes in. They also do interviews; host guest blog posts, and provide another high-traffic personal/book page for you to post samples and content. This equals more stuff to tweet, and more ways to be found.

More importantly than anything else, follow up your book with another novel, or at the very least a couple of short stories for sale (with links to your website and the sell pages of your novel at the end.) Even if they don't sell very much, you have more to tweet about. One thing about all of the successful indie authors I see is they all have a series or a few books out. One hit wonders will be hard to launch in this new ebook world.

*Another twitter hash tag tip:

If you are tweeting the Barnes and Noble link to your book, add the #Nook or #NookColor hash tag to your tweet.

If you are tweeting the Amazon link, add the #Kindle tag.

This a tweet of a link to a book review, so it can go out to all of the ereader tags:

"S.J. Wist's #BookReview of: 'The Sword and the Dragon' by M.R. Mathias http://t.co/Ip3Ol9F #Kindle #Nook #Sony #iPad #iPod #Smashwords #RT" This one Tweet will make it into 8 lists.

Here is one that is only relevant to Amazon:

"#FREE at Amazon for a limited time 'The First Dragoneer' a 43 page #fantasy novella by M.R. Mathias http://t.co/Fjltn5r via @Amazon #Kindle #iPad #Droid #RT"

The tags for #iPad and #Droid were added because Amazon has free Kindle reading apps for those devices. The tag for #fantasy was added because it is a fantasy book. #Romance #Thriller #Mystery and every other genre is hash tagged like this too. #HowTo #SelfHelp #Addiction, you name it.

Recap of Step Eight:

Continue the posting cycle. Use more hash tags to direct the tweets about your book/books. Write more books, short stories, and flash fiction to sell.

Step Nine

I have started using hash tags. I am writing the next masterpiece.

What do I do now?

Giveaways, contests, and blog advertising/blog touring is what you do. Contests on blogs are a good way to increase awareness. With the Smashwords coupon system, you can have a blogger give away several free copies of your eBook. Some bloggers will host giveaways for free. Everyone wants new followers and these virtual gatherings draw them. This is also a simple, free method to generate things to tweet and post about.

Cost: 3 free ebooks and some time.

Result: Curious, happy readers digging into your samples and profiles. New friends, followers, and fans. Sales. New links to tweet and post about. **Name Recognition.**

Several successful giveaways involve giving a kindle or nook away. It you have 1500 or more Twitter followers and a blog (or a blog willing to host you) this is the best bang for your buck. The blog's followers get a chance to win. You and the blogger both have something to tweet about. This draws in followers for both of you. In the end, you have spent $130 on a Kindle or Nook and gained a ton of name recognition and followers. A few months after the contest, do a guest post at the blog. When you do, you will no longer be an unknown. You will have **Name Recognition.**

Another thing you can do is set up an annual contest for charity. Every year, author L. M. Stull hosts my Dragon Poems for Smiletrain.org contest. (@LMStull on twitter) It will be huge this year. All entries get into the "profit for charity" anthology. That is available at B&N and Amazon.

Use your new found following for good, and good will come right back to you. Like I said before, Twitter Karma is a good thing to have.

After about **6 months** of continuing your cycle, you will have to face the facts. If you are still failing to sell books, either you are not keeping up your end of posting and tweeting, or your book isn't that good. **It's that simple.**

If this is the case, do not despair. Start over and use what you've learned to make the next attempt better. If the book failed miserably, take a new picture and use a different pen name. If you are seeing middling sales that's OK, some genres have a lot more competition. The next step can propel a good, well-reviewed book into the stratosphere. It's not recommended for authors whose books have a low starred review rating at Amazon and B&N, or small sales numbers.

Recap of step nine:

Work on new material and continue the posting cycle. Participate in giveaways, blog interviews, and submit your book for review at as many places as you can.

Step Ten

My book is actually selling.

What do I do now?

If you are selling over 100 ebooks a month at Amazon, you are doing something that about 85% of self publishers are failing to do. You need the next level, and you desperately need another book. Using only the money the book is generating, make, or have someone make, a banner ad for you.

Most Kindle/eReader/Book Review related blogs that have over a thousand regular followers have some sort of banner advertising or sponsorship spots in place. A lot of them will make the banner for you. If you don't see any ads at a blog, email the blog's owner and start a dialogue. Don't pay too much. $30 a day for a prime post on a well followed blog (over 1k followers) is the top of the range.

Remember, you could get three weeks worth of promo out of a $130 eReader giveaway. Do the math and try to figure what is best for you and your book.

Messaging sites such as eBookGabs, Kindle Boards, and Nook Boards sell the top of the page spots for a set rate. Goodreads has "pay-per-click" advertising that puts your book right in the face of real readers. $40 will go a long way, because your ad will be displayed 200 or 300 times for each click you have to pay for.

If you are selling well over 100 eBooks a month at Amazon and have not yet published with Createspace, then do so immediately. As soon as the book is proofed and approved, contact Publishers Weekly and pay to get the book listed in the Indie Showcase. This listing goes out to libraries, along with brick and mortar stores. You will also get a spot in the indie supplement that comes out quarterly. This type of pay promotion is most effective when there is a follow up novel, or a series already available.

Print magazines and online magazines sell ad space. Shop around. Don't try to sell 'Serial Killer Sally" in Cosmo. However, it would probably generate a bunch of sales with an ad in "Gore" magazine. **Shelf Unbound** is an awesome digital magazine for the indie world. Subscribe while it is still free. You'll learn what is trending, and what else is out there.

Always try to let the book pay its own way. If it needs a better cover, or an updated edit, get those things done **before you start spending big money** on advertising. Once the book gets into the top 100 of its genre at Amazon, let the list do the work. Tweets like this, when they are true, get the job done:

"The Sword and the Dragon (The Wardstone Trilogy Book One) by M. R. Mathias 10+ Months in the Amazon Fantasy Top 100 http://t.co/WHKzGQi #Kindle #RT"

Don'ts:

I do not recommend advertising with Foreward Magazine or Clarion review. For $300 they did "very little" for *The Butcher's Boy* by my other pen name, Michael Robb. @Michael_Robb on Twitter if you are interested. (See how I slipped that in there.)

Don't let other authors or nay-say-ers get you down. I judge my books by their own performance. I watch other books, and pay attention when they rise or fall in the charts. That's just smart.

- **Try to outsell your own last month.** Don't try to outsell another author.

If you follow these **Ten Steps** and keep to your cycle, the foundation for your future as an indie author will be stable. Your second and third books will boost the sale of your first book. Soon you will be worried about paying taxes on all the money you are making and answering fan email.

It's a brave, new world out there. Grab a hold of it and make it yours. Diligence, will power, and always remembering that you are your own publisher will take you far.

That's it. If you make it this far, you no longer need me.

Good luck,

M. R. Mathias, International Bestselling Author of:

The Wardstone Trilogy and *The Saga of the Dragoneers* series of books.

Find me at: (I realize that if you are reading this in paperback these links will be tedious.) ☺

The Wardstone Homepage: http://www.mrmathias.com/

The Dragoneers Homepage: http://www.mrmathias.com/Dragoneers.html

Twitter: main @DahgMahn, alternate @Michael_Robb, & @BookReTweeter

Facebook: https://www.facebook.com/#!/Author.M.R.Mathias

Goodreads:
http://www.goodreads.com/author/show/4163056.M_R_Mathias

Wattpad: http://www.wattpad.com/user/MRMathias

I.A.N.: http://www.independentauthornetwork.com/

Amazon: http://www.amazon.com/M.-R.-Mathias/e/B0040CD21I/

B&N: http://www.barnesandnoble.com/s/m-r-mathias

Smashwords:
http://www.smashwords.com/profile/view/MRMathias

If you want to contact me, do it via Goodreads messaging. I am online a good portion of every day and I will do my best to help you if I can. See you at the top of the charts!   **THE END**

www.ingramcontent.com/pod-product-compliance
Lightning Source LLC
Chambersburg PA
CBHW060935050326
40689CB00013B/3101